GW00374241

THE

O,

CORKMAN

JOKES

by

Des MacHale

THE MERCIER PRESS

THE MERCIER PRESS
P.O. Box 5, 5 French Church St., Cork.
24 Lower Abbey Street, Dublin 1.

ISBN 0 85342 478 0

Printed in Ireland by Litho Press Co., Midleton, Co. Cork.

INTRODUCTION

As I write these words my house is surrounded by a thousand members of the A.P.C.K.* who are armed with bodhrans, wild goats, and footballs. They will not lift the siege unless I supply them with a manuscript of several hundred Corkman jokes, designed to put Corkmen in their place once and for all.

To avoid unnecessary bloodshed I have written this book despite the difficult position in which it places me. Cork is my adopted county and I intend to spend the rest of my life here, heavily disguised of course. In addition, my three year old son, a full-blooded Corkman, will never forgive me when he is old enough to understand.

It will be very interesting to see how Corkmen, who have manufactured hundreds of Kerryman jokes over the last few years and laughed their sides sore repeating them to each other, will react to jokes about themselves. The idea of the Corkman joke is not new, because many Kerryman jokes often surface in Dublin as Corkman jokes, a consequence no doubt of the fact that there are probably more Corkmen in Dublin city than in Cork. Furthermore, as any Dubliner will tell you, Corkmen seem to be running the Capital.

Racial or regional jokes seem to be enjoying something of a boom at the moment. Many of the Corkmen and Kerrymen jokes have been undoubtedly inspired by the recent spate of anti-Irish jokes in England, but in my opinion the theory that the whole business started with Polack and Newfie jokes in North America or with Van der Merwe jokes in South Africa, has very little evidence to support it. A quick glance through the jokebooks of the last century will show that the anti-Irish 'Pat and Mike' and 'Bridget' jokes were rife in both England and America during that period and these very jokes often reappear, suitably modernised, as Polack, Newfie, or Van der Merwe jokes. If we go back to the seventeenth or eighteenth century, the Irish buffoon was often a figure of fun on the English stage and in English jest books.

*Association for the Prevention of Cruelty to Kerrymen.

Racial humour therefore, in my opinion, originated in these islands and we Irish have a proud record of being abused, insulted, and joked about.

Why does Ireland need a *Book of Corkman Jokes* at this point in her sad history? Well, as a recent letter to the newspapers pointed out, Corkmen definitely look upon themselves as superior to their fellow countrymen, and with good reason. Cork is the largest county in Ireland and has won as many Senior Hurling titles as any other county and is of course the home of the 'REAL Taoiseach'. A Corkman has variously been defined as a fellow who would get into a revolving door behind you and come out in front of you, a Welshman who couldn't swim, or a Kerryman with boots on. The fact that this book is being published in Cork by a Cork publisher shows that nobody can accuse Corkmen of taking themselves too seriously.

Finally, a word of advice. The modern joke is basically an explosive interpersonal acoustic experience, often encapsulated in riddle form. Almost invariably therefore, it loses its impact on the printed page, so if you want to enjoy these jokes at their best, read them aloud to your friends – there is no better way to get rid of friends. And remember, the world has never needed laughter so much – spread it **around**.

ACKNOWLEDGEMENT

THE PUBLISHER AND AUTHOR wish to thank CHARLES KELLY for his permission to use the *Dublin Opinion* cartoon.

If anyone can find a Corkman, living or dead, who remotely resembles the Corkmen in this book, I would very much like to meet him.

TO MY SON PETER

MY FAVOURITE CORKMAN

A Corkman rushed into a police station and told the sergeant that his car had just been stolen.

'Did you get a good look at the thief?' the sergeant asked.

'No'. said the Corkman, 'but I got his number'.

****

A little Cork village had just bought a new fire engine and the local councillors were wondering what should be done with the old one.

'I've got an idea', said one councillor, 'why not keep the old engine for false alarms?'

****

A Corkman set up a new photographic service but it didn't work out very well.

It was called 'Rent-a-Flash-Bulb'.

****

Have you heard about the Kerryman who sold a £10 parking ticket to a Corkman for £5?

****

A Corkman read about experiments showing that the tar and nicotine in cigarettes caused cancer in rats and mice. So he put all his cigarettes on the top shelf where the rats and mice couldn't get at them.

****

A Corkman went to America where he became a policeman. One night he had handed out a hundred and seventy-three parking tickets before he realised that it was a drive-in movie.

****

How do you recognise a Cork racing driver in a big race? He makes a hundred pit stops. Three for fuel, four for tyre changes, and ninety-three to ask for directions.

****

How do you recognise a Corkman well versed in etiquette?
He doesn't blow his soup – he fans it with his cap.

****

At the time of Ireland's entry to the Common Market it was felt that our custom of driving on the left-hand side of the road would be confusing to our European neighbours. A Corkman proposed a revolutionary new scheme to make our transition of driving on the other side of the road a little easier. He proposed that the change-over be made very gradually and that for the first few weeks it should apply to heavy lorries only.

****

A Corkman arrived at the gates of Heaven and was asked by St Peter where he was from.
'Cork', he replied proudly.
'Get to Hell out of here', said St Peter, 'surely you don't expect us to make drisheen for one'.

****

Have you heard about the Corkman who went to a mind reader?
He got his money back.

****

A new Institute for Advanced Mathematics has just been opened in Cork. Most popular courses are Fractions and Long Division.

****

Why has Australia got all the kangaroos and Cork got all the Corkmen?
Australia had the first choice.

****

Have you heard about the Cork grandmother who went on the pill?
She didn't want to have any more grandchildren.

****

Have you heard about the Corkman who thought that manual labour was a Spanish trade union official?

****

A Corkman once led from start to finish in the Olympic Marathon. However, he didn't get a medal because it was a false start.

****

Did you know that if a Corkman moves to Dublin he decreases the level of intelligence in both counties?

****

Cork's Coal Quay is one of the most colourful markets in the country and must be one of the few places where pounds, shillings, and pence are still talked about. One old lady in charge of her stall said that decimal currency would never catch on there and that it was particularly unfair on old people who had been used to the other system all their lives. 'Why didn't they wait until all the old people were dead before introducing it?' she asked.

****

Have you heard about the Cork pilot who had an accident with his helicopter?
He thought it was a bit cold so he turned the fan off.

****

A Corkman was sitting on his front doorstep dressed in pyjamas and dressing gown at three o'clock in the morning when a Guard passed by.
'What are you doing there?' asked the Guard.
'I'm waiting for the cat to come home, so I can put him out for the night', said the Corkman.

****

'I've had just about enough', said a Corkman to his wife, 'the only solution is for your mother to leave and find a place of her own'.
'My mother?' screamed his wife, 'I thought she was your mother'.

****

A Corkman visited a library and asked the assistant if he could recommend any plays for him to read.

'How about Shakespeare?' asked the assistant.

'I'll give him a try', said the Corkman, so the assistant gave him *The Complete Plays of William Shakespeare*.

Next day he returned saying that he had read the book and enjoyed it immensely.

'Do you have any more plays by the same author?' he asked the assistant.

For a joke, the assistant gave him a telephone directory to take home, so when the Corkman returned two days later the assistant asked him if he had enjoyed it.

'Well', said the Corkman, 'I didn't think much of the plot, but oh boy, what a cast'.

****

Have you heard about the Cork explorer who paid £10 for a sheet of sandpaper?

He thought it was a map of the Sahara Desert.

****

A Corkman bought a barometer and took it home but when he hung it up on the wall he found that it registered 'Hurricane'. So he took it back to the shop and complained, whereupon he was immediately given a replacement. When he arrived home he found that his house had been blown away.

****

It is notoriously difficult to get an appointment with a certain Cork publisher. A sign on his door says:

OFFICE HOURS   2 to 2:15
EVERY OTHER WEDNESDAY

****

An old lady asked a Cork tramp why he was dressed in such a miserable collection of rags.

'It's my unfortunate condition', he told her, 'there isn't a tailor in town who can measure me for a suit, I'm that ticklish'.

****

A Corkman who was 4 foot 3½ inches tall once offered his services to a well-known circus. He claimed he was the tallest dwarf in the world.

****

Have you heard about the Cork doctor who was treating a patient for jaundice for over three years?
He suddenly found out the fellow was Chinese. Worse still, he cured him.

****

There once was a Cork medical student who failed all his exams in surgery because he couldn't lance a boil properly. He kept falling off his horse.

****

A Corkman once visited his psychiatrist and told him that he thought he was turning into a packet of biscuits.
'What sort of biscuits?' asked the psychiatrist.
'Square ones', said the Corkman.
'With little holes in them?' asked the psychiatrist.
'Yes doc', said the Corkman with relief, 'That's it exactly'.
'You're crackers', said the psychiatrist.

****

Anybody who thinks that Corkman jokes and Kerryman jokes are all manufactured by malicious outsiders might like to know that the following announcement was read out over the public address system at a recent football match played in Cork between Cork and Kerry:
'Tickets are now on sale for a raffle which will be held at the interval. Tickets are priced 10p each or a book of four for 50p'.

****

A fellow was giving a Corkman a lift in his car but he didn't know if his indicators were working. So he asked the Corkman to go behind the car and tell him.
'Well', he shouted after a few seconds, 'are they working?'
'They are, they aren't, they are, they aren't', shouted the Corkman.

****

How can you recognise a superstitious Corkman?
He won't work during any week with a Friday in it.

****

Over the years the best supported flag days in Cork have been those for T.V. sets for the Blind and Radios for the Deaf.

****

What do you do if a Corkman throws a grenade at you?
Take out the pin and throw it back.

****

Three Corkmen went to America where they were immediately called up for Army service. In the hope of being exempted, each of them pleaded unfitness on medical grounds.

The first Corkman explained that he was shortsighted. He was sent right up to the front line where he would have no difficulty in seeing the enemy.

The second Corkman explained that one of his legs was shorter than the other. He was sent to fight on hilly ground.

The third Corkman decided to be more subtle – he had all his teeth extracted. He was exempted because he had flat feet.

****

What happens to a girl who goes out with a Corkman for an evening?
Nothing!

****

A Martian landed in West Cork right beside a farmer digging in a field.

'Take me to your leader', said the Martian, 'I'm from Mars'.

'I'm very pleased to meet you', said the Corkman, 'I've often meant to write and tell you how much I enjoy your chocolate bars'.

****

Have you heard about the Corkman who was taking his driving test?
He opened the car door to let the clutch out.

****

11

A Corkman came home unexpectedly to find a naked man in his bedroom.

'Don't worry darling', his wife reassured him, 'he's just a nudist who has come in to use the telephone'.

****

The following sign is displayed prominently in a Cork shop: CREDIT IS GIVEN ONLY TO THOSE OVER EIGHTY – PROVIDED THEY ARE ACCOMPANIED BY THEIR GRANDPARENTS.

****

Have you heard about the Corkman who got a job as quality control officer in a banana factory?

They had to sack him because he kept throwing away all the ones that were crooked.

****

Two Corkmen set up a furniture removal company. One afternoon they spent over an hour attempting to move a wardrobe which was wedged in a narrow stairway.

'It's no use', said the first Corkman, 'we'll never get it upstairs'.

'Upstairs?' said the second Corkman, 'I thought we were trying to get it downstairs'.

****

Have you heard about the Corkman who drove his car to Angola?

He wanted to insure it with the MPLA.

****

A Corkman once wrote to the *Guinness Book of Records* and claimed that he should be included. He explained that at one stage he had been the youngest person in the world.

****

Cork's G.P.O. is reputed to have had for many years a postbox bearing the following notice:–

FOR LETTERS TOO LATE FOR THE NEXT DELIVERY.

****

Two poteen makers from West Cork were on their first train journey. With them they had a pint bottle of poteen, fresh from the still. As the first Corkman raised the bottle to his lips and took a long drink, the train happened to pass through a tunnel.

'Don't touch that stuff', he shouted to the second Corkman, 'I've just been struck blind'.

****

Have you heard about the Corkman who bought a black and white dog?

He figured the licence would be cheaper than for a coloured one.

****

A Corkman went to a psychiatrist and told him that his wife thought she was a television set.

'Don't worry', said the psychiatrist, 'I'll soon cure her of that'.

'Oh I don't want you to cure her', said the Corkman, 'just adjust her to pick up BBC 1'.

****

How do you recognise an aircraft designed by a Corkman?
It has outside toilets.

****

Have you heard about the Corkman who took up water polo?
His horse got drowned.

****

Have you heard about the Corkman's dog who was sitting by the fire eating a bone?

When he got up he realised he had only three legs.

****

'My wife is most unreasonable', a Corkman told a marriage counsellor.

'Could you give me an example of her behaviour?' asked the counsellor.

'Yes', said the Corkman, 'only the other night I was having a bath when she burst into the bathroom and sank all my toy boats'.

****

13

A Corkman saw a sign outside a restaurant:

CHICKEN DINNERS 25p each.

So he went inside and ordered one. He was served with a dish of Indian meal.

****

One Corkman owed another £5 for over a year so he finally decided to pay up.

'Do you know', said the second Corkman, 'I'd completely forgotten that I had lent you that money'.

'If only you'd told me that', said the first Corkman, 'I could have saved myself £5'.

****

'Gentlemen of the jury', shouted the crier in a Cork court, 'please proceed to your accustomed places'.

The court erupted as the twelve Corkmen proceeded to cram themselves into the dock.

****

A Corkman's bicycle was stolen so he telephoned the Guards and reported the incident as follows:—

'I came out of the pub and there was my new bike up against the wall, gone'.

****

A Corkman and a Kerryman got jobs on a building site, the Corkman carrying a load of bricks and the Kerryman pushing a wheelbarrow. After a few weeks the Corkman complained to the foreman and said that he wanted to push a wheelbarrow like the Kerryman.

'What makes you think you can handle machinery?' asked the foreman.

****

How do you know if a Corkman and his wife are about to have a baby?

They put a Family Planning application notice in the newspapers.

****

A Corkman went into a restaurant in an area notorious for pickpockets and petty thefts. Seeing a notice:

WATCH YOUR COAT CAREFULLY.

he sat in a position where he had a clear view of the coatrack all through his meal. When he came outside he found his trousers were missing.

****

On seeing a lobster pot for the first time and having been told what it was called, a Corkman exclaimed, 'I don't believe it. How would you get a lobster to sit on one of those things?'

****

Have you heard about the Corkman who thought that aperatif was the French for a set of dentures?

****

What do you call a brick on a Corkman's head?
An extension.

****

A Corkman's wife gave birth to a baby weighing only one pound and four ounces. The doctors were amazed because the baby was perfectly healthy and thriving. 'It's not surprising really', explained the Corkman, 'we've only been married for three weeks'.

****

A Corkman was driving to Kerry for his holidays when he was stopped by a Guard late one evening.
'Excuse me sir', said the Guard, 'you don't seem to have any rear lights'.
'Never mind about my rear lights', said the Corkman, 'where's my caravan?'

****

What's the most popular dish on the menu in a restaurant owned by a Corkman?
Soup in the basket.

****

'Have you agreed on a decision?' the judge asked a Corkman who was foreman of a jury which had already been out for eight hours.

'Yes, your worship', replied the Corkman.

'Is your decision unanimous?' continued the judge.

'It is, your worship', replied the Corkman.

'And what is your decision?'

'That we send out for another barrel of porter'.

****

Two Corkmen were escaping from a well-protected jail at night. All they had with them was a flashlamp, so when they reached the forty-foot wall surrounding the jail one Corkman said to the other:

'I'll shine the flashlamp up to the top of the wall and you climb up along the beam'.

'Hold on', said the second Corkman, 'how do I know that you won't switch off the lamp when I am halfway up?'

****

Two Corkmen were discussing their childhood.

'When I was born', said the first Corkman, 'I weighed only four pounds'.

'That's astonishing', said the second Corkman, 'tell me, did you live?'

'Live?' said the first Corkman, 'you should see me now'.

****

Have you heard about the Irish speaking Corkman who had a relapse of measles?

It was a case of a rash arís.

****

A Corkman's explanation of why the sea is so salty — it's all those herrings swimming around.

****

Have you heard about the Cork psychiatrist who used to put his wife under the bed?

He thought she was just a little potty.

****

16

A Corkman came home early one afternoon and just as he came in the door the telephone rang so he answered it.
'Who was that dear on the phone?' shouted his wife from the kitchen.
'It was a wrong number, darling', said the Corkman, 'some fellow looking for the Met. Office. He wanted to know if the coast was clear'.

****

A Cork lawyer whose client was charged with murdering his father and mother by knocking their heads off with an axe opened his defence as follows:—
'Gentlemen of the jury, consider this poor orphan ...'

****

A Corkman has just invented a new labour-saving mouse-trap — it comes complete with its own mice.

****

What do you call a Corkman who is a sanitary expert?
Conn-a-sewer.

****

A Corkman got a job as coach to a well known English first division football side.
'When do I start to train the team?' he asked the manager.
'What do you mean "train the team"? ' asked the manager, 'you were hired to carry the team to away matches'.

****

A Corkman was explaining the mysteries of Science and Telecommunications to his little son. 'The telephone', he told him, 'is like a big dog with his tail in Cork and his head in Dublin. When you step on his tail in Cork, he barks in Dublin'.
'That's a wonderful explanation', said the little boy, 'now explain to me about the radio'.
'The radio is exactly the same, my son', said the Corkman, 'but without the dog'.

****

A Corkman rushed into a bank with a nylon stocking over his face, pointed a gun at the cashier and said, 'this is an up-stick'.
'Surely you mean it's a stick-up', said the cashier.
'Look', said the Corkman, 'don't confuse me, it's my first job'.

****

What do you find written on the bottom of Cork beer bottles?
Open other end.
What do you find written on the top of Cork beer bottles?
See other end for instructions.

****

How do you recognise a Corkman's roll of toilet paper?
Look for the instructions printed on every sheet.

****

A Corkman received a bill for £10 from his shoemaker so he sent the following reply:
'I never ordered those shoes, and if I did, you never sent them, and if you did, I never got them, and if I did, I paid for them, and if I didn't, I won't'.

****

A Corkman was asked by a salesman if he would like to buy a suitcase.
'What could I use it for?' asked the Corkman.
'Well, you could put your clothes in it', said the salesman.
'What', said the Corkman, 'and go naked?'

****

Have you heard about the Cork girl who came second in a beauty contest?
She was the only entrant.

****

'The fellow who would stoop so low', said a Corkman, 'as to write an anonymous letter, the very least he might do is to sign his name to it'.

****

What does a Corkman do if he gets a hole in his sock?
He turns the sock inside out.

****

What does a Cork fatted calf say when he sees the Prodigal Son coming over the hill?
O goody, here comes the Prodigal Son.

****

A Corkman's coat fell down a sewer so he spent half an hour trying to fish it out again.
A man passing by suggested that he abandon the coat because even if he got it out, it would never be fit to wear again.
'Oh I know that', said the Corkman, 'but there were three sandwiches in the pocket'.

****

A Corkman became an undertaker but had to close down his business after a few weeks. It seems that little boys were driving him crazy coming in asking for empty boxes.

****

How does a Corkman do a 'Spot the Ball' entry?
He prods around his newspaper with a pin until he hears 'psst'.

****

Two Corkmen were talking in a pub.
'I wouldn't go to America if you paid me', said the first Corkman.
'Why is that?' asked the second.
'Well for one thing, they all drive on the right hand side of the road there'.
'And what's wrong with that?' inquired the second Corkman.
'Well I tried it driving to Dublin the other day and it's terrible'.

****

'Show me a place', said a Corkman, 'where nobody dies, and I'll go and end my days there'.

****

What's the best thing that ever came out of Cork?
The road to Dublin.

****

This fellow met a Corkman wearing only one shoe.
'What's the matter', he asked him, 'have you lost a shoe?'
'No', said the Corkman, 'I've just found one'.

****

A Corkman invented a new diet guaranteed to make anybody lose 14 lbs in a week. It consisted of eating nothing else except dripping. He had heard the old proverb 'constant dripping wears a stone'.

****

A Cork undertaker called at a house to collect a client. Not being sure of the address he asked the woman who answered the doorbell: 'Is this where the man that's dead lives?'

****

A Guard in a country village was astonished to see a fellow walking along the road with a huge TO DUBLIN roadsign under his arm, so he asked him to explain what he was doing. 'I'm a Corkman walking to Dublin', said the fellow, 'and I don't want to lose my way'.

****

A Corkman who lived in a remote mountain village was awoken one morning by the postman delivering a letter. 'You shouldn't have come all that way just to bring me one letter', said the Corkman, 'why didn't you post it?'

****

A Corkman was condemned to receive forty lashes but the more they whipped him the more he laughed.
'What's so funny?' they asked him.
'You don't understand', he told them, helpless with laughter. 'you're whipping the wrong man'.

****

20

A Corkman got a job as assistant in a hotel kitchen and was given the task of filling all the salt cellars. After a few hours he was asked if he had finished but replied that he had only managed to fill one.

'It's the devil's own job putting the salt in through that little hole at the top', he added.

****

Have you heard about the Corkman whose canary lost it's sight in an accident?

He took it to the Bird's Eye factory.

****

A Cork detective had just taken a much wanted criminal into custody when his cap blew off. 'Do you want me to go and get it for you?' asked the prisoner obligingly.

'You must think I'm a right fool', said the Corkman, 'you stand here while I go and get it'.

****

A Corkman was paying his annual visit to the dentist. 'Your teeth are fine', the dentist told him, 'but your gums will have to come out'.

****

Have you heard about the Corkman who thought Yoko Ono was Japanese for one egg?

****

A Cork travel agent looked out through his window to see an old lady and an old man gazing longingly at his display of posters for exotic holiday resorts. As a publicity gimmick he decided to offer them a free round-the-world cruise with all expenses paid.

When they returned some months later he asked the old lady if they had enjoyed themselves. 'Wonderfully', she replied, 'but tell me one thing, who was that old man I had to sleep with every night?'

****

Have you heard about the Corkman who spent two hours buying a cap in a department store?
He was looking for one with a peak at the back.

****

A Corkman once set out to swim the Channel. However, when he was about three-quarters of the way across he felt he wouldn't make it, so he turned round and swam home.

****

How many Corkmen does it take to carry out a kidnapping?
Ten — one to capture the kid and nine to write the ransom note.

****

Have you heard about the Corkman who bought a bunch of artificial flowers?
He went back to the shop trying to buy artificial water.

****

Have you heard the sad story of the Corkman who was a haemophiliac?
He tried to cure himself by acupuncture.

****

A Corkman became one of the world's leading surgeons. The highlight of his career came when he carried out the first appendix transplant.

****

First Corkman: 'I see where Murphy has just run a hundred metres in six seconds'.
Second Corkman: 'That's impossible, the world record is over nine seconds'.
First Corkman: 'Murphy found a shortcut'.

****

How do you recognise a Corkman's cuckoo clock?
Every twenty-five minutes the cuckoo pops its head out and asks what time it is.

****

A Corkman got a job working in a storeroom and the first assignment he was given was to put THIS END UP labels on a few hundred crates.

'Have you managed to do it?' the foreman asked him a little later.

'Yes', said the Corkman, 'and in case they couldn't be seen on the top, I've put them on the bottom as well'.

****

How do you sink a submarine designed by a Corkman? Put it in water.

****

A Corkman joined the army and after three years service was awarded the special crossed knife and fork ensignia. This was to celebrate three years of eating with a knife and fork without accident.

****

An old West Corkman and his wife were on a visit to Dublin. They decided to have a meal at an expensive restaurant where they ordered a four-course dinner with steak as the main course.

When the meal was served the West Corkman tucked in while his wife sat looking at her plate for over ten minutes. 'Isn't the meal to your satisfaction madam?' asked the head waiter.

'Certainly it is', said the old lady with relish, 'but I'm waiting for Pa to finish with the teeth'.

****

A successful Cork businessman was boasting about how poor his family had been when he was a child.

'For the first five years', he claimed, 'I hadn't a stitch to wear. Then when I was six my mother bought me a cap and I used to sit looking out the window'.

****

A Corkman was on his first visit to the zoo. He was annoyed because he followed the sign LADIES but they were all locked in their cages where he couldn't see them.

****

THE ORIGINAL CORKMAN JOKE

...Y WAS SIGNED ◦

DUBLIN OPINION 1924

An interesting fact about this huge canvas is that it was painted almost entirely from living models, many of whom participated in the original Gold Rush.

The third from the right in the extreme top corner is now a principal officer in the Department of F- - - - ce on a salary scale of £815 to £915 a year, exclusive of bonus. Though badly placed at the Macroom bend, he gained ground rapidly on the straight Tipperary stretch and drawing into the lead passing through Naas was never afterwards headed.

Mr. Eustace O'Honovan, who occupies third place in the picture, dropped back to almost last soon after passing Monasterevan and the best he could do was a clerical officer-ship in the Department of Posts and Telegraphs.

Mr. Herbert O'Twomey, who is seen in the lead in the picture, kept up a rare bat all the way till coming into Lucan when his wooden leg and the wind resistance to his nightgown began to tell against him. However, he finished a creditable sixth and secured a Junior Administrative post shortly after the abolition of the Entrance Examination for the position.

The gentleman who is seen in the picture taking the short cut over the wall and across the fields, ran into second place passing Sallins, but failed to overhaul the leader. He secured a £900 to £975 position in the Land Commission and, five hours after his appointment, sent home for his brother, only to find that the latter had secured a seat up on a lorry and had already established himself in the Office of Public Works.

Nothing definite is known of the official history of the Mr. M. O'Keeffe who is seen extricating himself from an awkward position on the left of the picture, but a friend of ours who addressed an appeal recently to the Revenue Department is of the opinion that the reply he got was from him.

A Corkman arrived home late one night in a state of more than mild intoxication. 'Where have you been?' asked his wife. 'I don't know', said the Corkman, 'but wherever it was it was terribly posh – they even had a golden toilet'.

Next morning a fellow called round looking for compensation for his damaged saxaphone.

****

Have you heard about the Corkman who used to use barbed wire for garters?

He wanted to keep his calves in.

****

A Corkman was lecturing about his travels in foreign countries. 'I came across a peculiar custom among the Chinese', he told his audience. 'If a rich man was condemned to death, he could save his life by paying somebody to die in his place. Many of the poor people made their living by acting as substitutes in this way'.

****

A Cork traffic warden explained the system of yellow lines on city streets as follows:–

One yellow line means no parking at all.

Two yellow lines mean no parking at all at all.

****

A Cork blacksmith gave the following instructions to his youthful assistant:–

'I'll put the red-hot iron on the anvil and when I nod my head you hit it'.

****

A Corkman was doing an examination to join the Civil Service. One question read:

Give first names of each of the following, STALIN, HITLER and GANDHI.

The Corkman wrote:–

I don't know about the first two but the answer to the third is Goosey Goosey.

****

A neurotic Kerryman is one who thinks that $2 + 3 = 6$.
A neurotic Corkman is one who knows that $2 + 3 = 5$ and
worries about it all the time.

****

Two Corkmen were waiting at a bus stop. When the bus drew
up it turned out to be a one-man bus so one Corkman turned
to the other and said:
'You can take this bus, I'll wait for the next one'.

****

A Corkman sent his son to University and after some time the
lad was awarded a B.A. degree. On graduation he received the
following telegram from his father:—
'Congratulations on getting your B.A. Now for the other
24 letters and this time for goodness sake get them in the right
order'.

****

Have you heard about the Corkman who decided to have
only three children?
He heard that one in every four children born is Chinese.

****

A Corkman was on the Mailboat to Holyhead when a man
fell overboard.
'Help', he shouted as he struggled in the water, 'drop me a line'.
'I can't', said the Corkman, 'I don't know your address'.

****

How do you recognise a Corkman staying in a big hotel?
He's the one trying to slam the revolving door.

****

Once upon a time there were two Corkmen — now look how
many there are.

****

A Cork barber displayed the following notice:
        HAIRCUTS WHILE YOU WAIT.

****

Two Cork bank clerks bought self-winding watches. One afternoon one bank clerk said to the other, 'these self-winding watches aren't much good Fergal. Mine's stopped'.

****

A Corkman went to his dentist and told him to take all his teeth out. When the dentist had extracted the last tooth the Corkman burst out laughing and said, 'April fool, I only wanted a haircut'.

****

Have you heard about the Corkman who thought that Chou-en-Lai was Chinese for bed and breakfast?

****

Have you heard about the Corkwoman who was ironing her husband's socks?
She burned his feet.

****

A Cork newspaper once carried the following notice on its front page:
'Today we present our prize crossword, first prize £1,000. But for those of you who want to do it just for fun and don't want to wait until next week for the answers, the solution is on the back page'.

****

A pilot in a single seat jet fighter once ran into difficulties when flying over West Cork. Seeing that the aircraft was on fire, he used the ejector seat to bale out. Two West Cork farmers were looking up at the scene. One turned to the other and said, 'Mick what will they think of next? I'm sure that was a flying toasting machine'.

****

Have you heard about the Corkman who thought that a barbecue was a line of people outside a gents hairdressers?

****

Two Corkmen were pushing a car up a hill and after an hour they finally made it.

'I thought we would never manage it', said the first Corkman. 'It's a good job that I remembered to leave the handbrake on', said the second Corkman, 'or it would have rolled downhill'.

****

Have you heard about the Cork kidnapper who was picked up by the police?

He enclosed a stamped addressed envelope with the ransom note.

****

A Corkman started a fantastic new sweepstake with a first prize of a million pounds − £1 a year for a million years.

****

A Corkman was given a present of a new boomerang. It took him over a month to throw the old one away.

****

A Corkman had two chickens and one of them became ill. So he killed the healthy chicken to make soup for the other one.

****

How can we be sure that Santa Claus is a Corkman? There are two doors in the average house and eight windows and he goes down the chimney.

****

Two Corkmen met on a train.

'Surely I know you', said the first Corkman, 'didn't we meet in Dublin about three years ago?'

'I've never been to Dublin', said the second Corkman. 'Neither have I', said the first Corkman, 'it must have been two other fellows'.

****

Have you heard about the Corkman with a serious problem? He thought he had a bigger and better inferiority complex than anybody else in the world.

****

A Jury consisting of twelve Corkmen once returned the following verdict:-

'We find the defendant guilty as charged. We admit he didn't do it because he was somewhere else at the time, but we think he would have done it if he had the chance'.

****

How does a Corkman cook sausages?
First he guts them and then he skins them.

****

'What are my chances of surviving this operation?' a Corkman asked his doctor.

'Excellent', said the doctor, 'nine out of ten patients die under this operation and the last nine patients I have operated on have died'.

****

'Why did you steal £100,000?' the judge asked a Corkman who had pleaded guilty to robbery. 'I was hungry, your honour', replied the Corkman.

****

'I hear that your husband had a post-mortem operation', said one Corkwoman to another. 'Yes', replied the second Corkwoman, 'but not until after he was dead. If only they had done it a bit earlier it might have saved his life'.

****

A Corkman explained the fact that cream is more expensive than milk as follows:—

Cream is dearer because they find it harder to make the cows sit on the smaller bottles.

****

What goes putt-putt-putt-putt.........?
A Cork golfer.

****

Two Cork labourers wandering aimlessly across their site were asked by the foreman where they were going and what they were doing.

'We're carrying these planks to the other end of the site', they told him.

'What planks?' he asked them.

'Will you look at that', said one Corkman to the other, 'we've forgotten the planks'.

****

How many Corkmen does it take to change a light bulb? A hundred — one to hold the bulb and ninety-nine to turn the room around.

****

A Corkman with more than a drop taken, arrived home at 4 a.m. wondering how he could get up to bed without waking his wife. Suddenly he had a bright idea. Tying all the pots and pans from the kitchen to a piece of string he proceeded to drag them upstairs.

'She'll never hear me with all this racket', he chuckled to himself.

****

Have you heard about the Corkman who committed suicide by drinking a can of varnish?

He had a terrible end but a beautiful finish.

****

'What are you buying your wife for her birthday?' one Corkman asked another.

'Some toilet water', said the second Corkman, 'but I'm told it's very expensive — up to £5 a bottle'.

'Why don't you come home to my house', said the first Corkman, 'and you can have all you want for free'.

****

Have you heard about the Corkman who became a streaker? He ran fully clothed through a nudist colony.

****

Two Corkmen wanted to make some money so they bought a lorryload of turnips at tenpence each. They sold the turnips at tenpence each and when they counted the proceeds they were amazed to find that they had exactly the same amount of money as they started with.

'See', said the first Corkman to the other, 'I told you we should have bought a bigger lorry'.

****

A Cork clergyman spent half an hour preaching to his congregation telling them that the church needed a chandelier. Afterwards a delegation of parishioners called to see him and gave three reasons why they should not buy a chandelier. 'Firstly', he said, 'some of us can't even spell chandelier. Secondly, there's nobody in the parish who can play it, and thirdly, what our church really needs is more light'.

****

Have you heard about the Cork photographer who used to save all his burned out light bulbs?
He used them in his darkroom.

****

Why do Corkmen make the best secret agents?
Even under torture they can't remember what they have been assigned to do.

****

Two Kerrymen decided to kidnap a little Cork boy. Two days after the kidnapping they sent the little lad home to his parents with a ransom note. Next day the parents sent him back with the ransom money.

****

A Corkman invented the world's most advanced burglar alarm. Unfortunately before he had time to patent it, it was stolen.

****

A Corkman when stopped by the Customs at Holyhead was found to be carrying two big bags of telephones.
'Could you explain what these are to be used for?' asked a Customs official. 'Certainly', said the Corkman. 'I've just got a job with the London Symphony Orchestra and they told me to bring two sacks of phones with me when I was coming to England'.

****

How does a Corkman cure water on the brain?
A tap on the head.
How does a Corkman cure water on the knee?
Drainpipe trousers.

****

Have you heard about the Corkman who joined the Mafia? They made him an offer he couldn't understand!

****

During a murder trial in Cork in the nineteenth century there was a sensation when the man who was supposed to have been murdered actually turned up in the courtroom. The judge immediately ordered the jury, consisting of twelve Corkmen, to return a verdict of 'not guilty'. After an hour the jury returned and the foreman announced that they had found the defendant guilty.
'How on earth could you reach such a verdict', asked the judge, 'when the supposed murdered man is here in court?'
'Yes, we know that your honour', answered the foreman, 'but we think the defendant is the man who stole my brother's horse two years ago'.

****

'How did Mrs. O'Sullivan's appendix operation go?' a Cork doctor was asked by his nurse.
'Appendix operation? ' he screamed, 'I was told it was a post-mortem'.

****

A Corkman on a visit to Dublin decided to send a surprise birthday gift to his wife at home in Cork. So he rang Interparrot and told them to send her a parrot that could speak seven different languages. When he arrived home that night he found that she had plucked the parrot and roasted it. 'You fool', he screamed at her, 'that bird spoke seven languages'.

'Well why didn't he say something before I put him in the oven?' she answered.

****

A Corkman was being charged with driving down the middle of the road. In defence he stated that one of the instructions in his driving test application form had been 'tear along the dotted line'.

****

One Corkman was explaining to another some of the basic theory of thermodynamics. 'Heat expands and cold contracts', he told him.

'I understand perfectly', said the second Corkman, 'how else could you explain why the days are longer in Summer and shorter in Winter?'

****

Three Corkmen were caught up in the French Revolution and were sentenced to be guillotined. As the first Corkman waited for the blade to fall, it stuck, and he was released according to the old custom. The same thing happened to the second Corkman and he too was released.

As the third Corkman looked up waiting for the blade he shouted out: 'Hold on, I think I can see what's making it stick'.

****

A Cork bank robber was picked up with a sawn-off shotgun. It seems he had sawn off the wrong end of the shotgun.

****

A Corkman who had just arrived in Dublin from a remote village wanted to send a telegram to his mother telling her of his safe arrival.

'The telegram will cost £2', said the clerk, 'plus a further charge of £1 for delivery'.

'Hang the delivery charge', said the Corkman, 'I'll write her a letter telling her to call and collect it at the post office'.

****

A Corkman who was fined £10 for being drunk and disorderly told the judge that he had no money to pay the fine. 'You would if you hadn't spent it on drink', the judge told him.

****

Have you heard about the Corkman who wrote to the Gay Byrne Hour asking him to speak up a bit because the batteries on his transistor radio were running down?

****

Why do Cork workers never go on strike?
Nobody would notice the difference.

****

Have you heard about the Cork chess champion? When he was only ten he played blindfold against twelve Soviet Grand Masters simultaneously. He was annihilated in all twelve matches.

****

A old story tells of a Corkman discovering a dead highwayman lying on the roadside with a small bullet hole in his left temple. The Corkman commented: 'Wasn't it the mercy of God that it didn't hit the poor fellow in the eye?'

****

Have you heard about the lucky Corkman?
He was always finding 10p pieces under plates in restaurants.

****

Have you heard about the Corkwoman who wanted to print HAPPY BIRTHDAY on her little boy's birthday cake? She spent half an hour trying to put the cake into her typewriter.

****

Have you heard about the Corkman who never took his wife anywhere?
It seems that his mother had warned him not to go out with married women.

****

A Corkwoman went upstairs one night to find her husband standing in front of a mirror with his eyes closed.
'I'm trying to see what I look like when I'm asleep', he explained.

****

Have you heard about the Corkman who spent three hours in a carwash?
He thought it was raining too hard to drive.

****

A Corkman got a job as a lift operator but was sacked after a week.
He couldn't remember his route.

****

How do you recognise a Corkman's pencil?
It's got an eraser at both ends.

****

A Corkman wanted to post a garden hose. He arrived up at the Post Office carrying a box one inch by one inch by fifty yards.

****

Have you heard about the Corkman who had to take a milk bath?
He couldn't find a cow tall enough to take a shower under.

****

A Corkman bought a genuine Rembrandt for £20.
'It's one of the few works he did in ballpoint', he told his friends proudly.

****

What's gross ignorance?
144 Corkmen.

****

'Did you hear the sad story about poor McCarthy?' one Corkman asked another. 'No', said the second Corkman, 'what happened to him?'
'A big steam hammer dropped forty feet onto his chest and killed him'.
'I'm not surprised', said the second Corkman, 'McCarthy always had a weak chest'.

****

Why do Cork Guards always travel in threes?
One who can read, one who knows how to make telephone calls, and the third a Special Branch man to keep an eye on two such dangerous intellectuals.

****

A Cork surgeon took his suit back to the tailor and complained.
'What's the matter with it?' asked the tailor.
'I don't know', said the surgeon, 'it was all right until I took the stitches out'.

****

A Corkman walked into a pub with a big front door under his arm.
'What are you doing with that door?' the barman asked.
'Well', said the Corkman, 'last night I lost the key, so in case anybody finds it and breaks into my house I'm carrying the door around'.
'But what happens if you lose the door?'
'That's O.K.', grinned the Corkman, 'I've left a window open'.

****

A Corkman once invented a foolproof cure for seasickness — sit under a tree.

****

A five-foot Corkman saw an ad. in the paper - *Increase your height for £10 - results guaranteed.* So he sent away £10 and received by return of post a long thin parcel containing a pair of stilts.

****

One Corkman met another who was screaming with pain.
'What's the matter with you?' he asked.
'I burned my finger in hot water', he replied.
'Why the heck didn't you feel the water before you put your hand in?' asked the second Corkman.

****

A very ugly Corkman claimed that he had been born a beautiful baby but had been exchanged at birth by a spiteful nurse.

****

A Corkman sent his son to University and a few days later received a letter from him asking for £10. To save face he added the following P.S.:
'I am so ashamed to ask you for money that I have run after the postman to recover this letter but the post had already gone. I can only pray that the letter will be lost in the post'.
A few days later he received the following letter from his father.
Dear Son,
Don't upset yourself, the letter was lost in the post.
                    Your loving father.

P.S. I would enclose the £10 but I have already sealed the envelope.

****

What does a Corkman take for a headache?
Nothing — because nothing acts faster than Anadin.

****

One Corkwoman was sympathising with another on the death of her husband. 'I believe he met his death by falling from a high building', she said.

'Yes', was the reply, 'he fell from the seventh storey'. 'Was it as bad as that?' asked the other Corkwoman, 'I heard it was only the fourth storey'.

****

Have you heard about the Corkman who arrived up at the telephone exchange with his black telephone and asked if he could have a blue one instead?

****

A Corkman was asked to suggest names for his sister's newly born twins, one a boy and other a girl. He came up with Denise and Denephew.

****

Have you heard about the Cork builder who fell into a lot of money?
He bought a JCB GXL.

****

A Cork carpenter fell sixty feet from the top of a building on which he was working. As they picked him up he told them philosophically, 'I had to come down for nails anyway'.

****

Have you heard about the Corkman who bought a pool table?
He filled it with water.

****

Three Corkmen were flying to Africa to work as labourers on the Aswan Dam. First they crossed the Mediterranean Ocean, so the first Corkman shouted out, 'will you look at all that water'. Next they crossed the Sahara Desert, so the second Corkman shouted out, 'will you look at all that sand'. 'Yes', said the third Corkman, 'let's turn back before they get the cement'.

****

Three Corkmen were caught up in the French Revolution and were sentenced to death. They were allowed to choose between the guillotine and hanging.

The First Corkman chose the guillotine but just as the blade was about to fall, it stuck. According to the old custom he was released.

The same thing also happened to the second Corkman. When the third Corkman's turn came he chose hanging,saying: 'That damn guillotine doesn't seem to be working at all'.

****

Have you heard about the Corkman whose horse broke a leg? He went home and covered it with treacle.

****

A Corkman got a job on a building site but the foreman was not satisfied with the amount of work he was doing. One afternoon he came across the Corkman digging in a pit. He ordered the Corkman to get out of the pit and the Corkman complied.

'Now get back in again', he told him. After this had happened half-a-dozen times the Corkman said, 'look, what the heck are you playing at?'

'That's better', said the foreman, 'you're taking more out on your boots than you were throwing out with your shovel'.

****

Have you heard about the Corkman who lost £10 on the Grand National?

Worse still, he lost £15 on the television rerun.

****

A Corkman started a new Dial-a-Weather-Forecast service. He advertised as follows:

    Dial 12718 for a sunny forecast.

    Dial 12940 for a rainy forecast.

****

Have you heard about the Corkman who went around taking up a collection for the widow of the Unknown Soldier?

****

A Cork nurse rushed into her ward and asked a seriously ill patient if he would mind jumping up and down on his bed. 'Why do you want me to do that?' he asked feebly. 'I forgot to shake your medicine before I gave it to you after lunch', she told him.

****

A Corkman phoned the Guards and told them to come immediately because the steering wheel, the gear lever, the clutch, the brake, and the accelerator of his car had all been stolen.

A few minutes later he rang again and told them not to bother coming because he had got into the back seat by mistake.

****

Have you heard about the Corkman who cut a hole in his umbrella?

He wanted to be able to tell when it had stopped raining.

****

A Corkman bet £10 that he could lean further out of a fourth storey window than a Kerryman. He won the bet.

****

A Corkman was in court charged with stealing a horse. 'You have a choice', the judge told him. 'You can be tried by me alone or by a jury of your peers'.

'What do you mean by "peers"?' asked the Corkman. 'Peers are your equals, men of your own kind and class'. 'Try me yourself judge', said the Corkman, 'I don't want to be tried by a bunch of horse thieves'.

****

In what month do Corkmen drink the least beer?
February.

****

How do you recognise a Cork intellectual?
He doesn't move his lips when he reads.

****

Have you heard about the Corkman who heard that 90% of car accidents happened within five miles of home? He moved house.

****

A Corkman's girlfriend decided to take the plunge and propose. 'Let's get married, darling', she suggested, 'and have three children'.
'Right', said the Corkman, 'we'll have one of each'.

****

A Corkman received a hundred dollars from his uncle in America to celebrate the bicentennial.
'These bicentennials are a great idea', said the Corkman, 'they should have one every year'.

****

Yet another Corkman was captured in the French Revolution and was sentenced to death by guillotine. Just as the blade was about to fall a letter arrived from the authorities containing a pardon.
'Throw it in the basket', said the Corkman, 'I'll read it later'.

****

A Kerryman and a Corkman were taking an intelligence test. 'What bird does not build its own nest?' the examiner asked.
'The canary', said the Kerryman, 'he lives in a cage'.
'The cuckoo', said the Corkman.
'Very good', said the examiner to the Corkman, 'how did you know?'
'Everybody knows the cuckoo lives in a clock', said the Corkman.

****

A poor Corkman was so hard up that he had to sell his only possession – a saucepan. He explained, 'I only sold it to buy something to put in it'.

****

A Corkman was charged with murder but was acquitted by the skin of his teeth. Afterwards he told his lawyer that he could prove he was innocent because he was in jail at the time the crime was committed.

'Why on earth didn't you tell that to the court?' asked his lawyer.

'I thought that it might prejudice the jury against me', said the Corkman.

****

A Corkman wanted to buy a box of matches so he went into the shop and asked for some free samples. The man in the shop gave him a box with three matches in it.

He tried to light the first but failed and the same thing happened when he tried to light the second. The third one however, lit immediately. 'This seems like a good one', he said, 'I'll keep this one'.

****

Cork is said to have the lowest mortality rate in the country. The reason is that most people wouldn't be found dead there.

****

A competition was organised to find a motto for Blarney Castle. It was won by a Corkman who submitted the following entry:

PÓG MO STONE

****

What's the longest one-way street in the world?
The road from Cork to Dublin.

****

How do you confuse a Corkman?
Put him in a barrel and tell him to stand in a corner.

****

EXAMINATION TO BECOME A MAYOMAN

Lest it be suggested that I am unable to joke about my native county (of which I am inordinately proud, God help us) let me present you with the examination which outsiders must first pass before they can become honorary Mayomen.

PART I (WRITTEN)

INSTRUCTIONS TO CANDIDATES

(a)   Do not attempt to answer more than one question at a time.

(b)   Do not attempt to write on both sides of the paper at the same time.

(c)   On no account attempt Question 3.

(d)   Slide Rules O.K.

N.B.   Candidates caught cheating will be given extra marks for initiative.

All candidates are requested to use separate answer books.

Time Allowed : 6 weeks

1.   Who won the Second World War? Who came second?

2.   Explain in one sentence Einstein's Theory of Relativity OR write your name in block capitals.

3.   What is the number of this question?

4.   Name the odd man out: The Chief Rabbi, The Pope, Jack the Ripper, The Archbishop of Canterbury.

5.   At the Irish Sheepdog Trials of 1972, how many sheepdogs were found guilty?

6.　At what time is the nine o'clock news broadcast?

7.　Spell each of the following words: DOG, CAT, PIG.

8.　Write a tongue twister three times quickly.

9.　There have been six kings of England named George. The latest was George the Sixth — name the other five.

10.　Quote four lines from any poem written in the English language or from any other poem written in the English language.

N.B.　This is the honours paper — there is a special pass version for Kerrymen.

****

PART II (PRACTICAL)

Leave the examination hall and persuade the first passer-by you meet to accompany you through life, using irony where necessary.

CORKMEN HIT BACK

Hell hath no fury like a Corkman scorned and traditionally his wrath has been directed towards Dubliners. Here then is a sample of what may hit the capital if Dubliners do not behave themselves.

What do you call a dead Dubliner?
A jack in the box.

****

Why are Corkman jokes so simple?
So Dubliners can understand them.

****

Why is the wheelbarrow the greatest of all human inventions?
It taught Dubliners to walk on their hind legs.

****

What is coloured light blue and lies at the bottom of Cork Harbour?
A Dubliner found telling Corkman jokes.

****

What did God say when he made his second Dubliner?
'I must be losing my touch'.

****

How do you tell the age of a Dubliner?
Cut off his head and count the rings.

****

What is the difference between a Dubliner and a ham sandwich?
The average ham sandwich is only half an inch thick.

****

Why do so many Dubliners have scratched faces?
From trying to eat with forks.

****

How do you keep Dubliners out of your house?
Hide the key under a bar of soap.

****

A Dubliner went to live in Cork but unfortunately he died. Two Corkmen went around from house to house collecting money to give him a decent funeral.
'Excuse me, Sir', they asked one old Corkman, 'would you contribute £1 to bury a Dubliner? '
'Look', said the Corkman, 'here's £10 − bury ten of them'.

****

A Dubliner on holiday in the country found three bottles of milk in a field. He thought he had discovered a cow's nest.

****

How do you recognise the bride at a Dublin wedding?
She's the one wearing the white maternity dress.

****

Why do Dubliners have big noses?
Dubliners have big fingers.

****

Two Dublin trade unionists were discussing the beauties of nature and the coming of spring.
'I see that the snowdrops are out', said one. 'How will that affect us? ' asked the other.

****

MORE MERCIER BESTSELLERS

THE BOOK OF CHILDRENS JOKES :
Mary Feehan.

BUMPER BOOK OF KERRYMAN JOKES :
Des McHale.

BALLADS FROM THE PUBS OF IRELAND :
James N. Healy.

IRISH PROVERBS & SAYINGS :
Padraic O'Farrell.

SUPERSTITIONS OF THE IRISH COUNTRY
PEOPLE :
Padraic O'Farrell.

THE BOOK OF IRISH CURSES :
Patrick C. Power.

IRISH FAIRY STORIES FOR CHILDREN :
Edmund Leamy.

IRISH FOLK STORIES FOR CHILDREN :
T. Crofton Croker.

IN MY FATHER'S TIME :
Eamon Kelly.

LETTERS OF A SUCCESSFUL T.D. :
John B. Keane.

LETTERS OF A LOVE HUNGRY FARMER :
John B. Keane.

A HISTORY OF IRISH FAIRIES :
Carolyn White.

THE BOOK OF KERRYMAN JOKES :
Des McHale.

JOKES FROM THE PUBS OF IRELAND :
James N. Healy.

THE WORST KERRYMAN JOKES :
Des McHale.

OFFICIAL KERRYMAN JOKE BOOK :
Des McHale.

THE BOOK OF KERRYMAN RIDDLES :
Sonnie O'Reilly.

THE BOOK OF DUBLINMAN JOKES :
Y. M. Hughes.

MORE KERRYMAN JOKES :
Des McHale.

IRISH LOVE AND MARRIAGE JOKES
Des McHale

THE BOOK OF KERRYWOMAN JOKES :
Laura Stack.

THE BOOK OF IRISH LIMERICKS :
Myler McGrath.